HIDE AND SHRIEK

Riddles about Ghosts & Goblins

by Jeffie Ross Gordon
pictures by Susan Slattery Burke

L Lerner Publications Company · Minneapolis

To our mummies, Ellenore and Sylvia, with love   —J.R.G.

To my wonderful daughter, Shea, for her incredible inspiration in this first year of her life   —S.S.B.

This book is available in two editions:
Library binding by Lerner Publications Company
Soft cover by First Avenue Editions
241 First Avenue North
Minneapolis, MN 55401

Library of Congress Cataloging-in-Publication Data

Gordon, Jeffie Ross.
   Hide and shriek : riddles about ghosts and goblins / by Jeffie Ross Gordon ; pictures by Susan Slattery Burke.
      p.   cm.
   Summary: Presents riddles about ghosts and goblins, such as "What do little ghosts do before bedtime? They take boo-ble baths."
   ISBN 0-8225-2336-1 (lib. bdg.)
   ISBN 0-8225-9594-X (pbk.)
   1. Riddles, Juvenile. 2. Ghosts—Juvenile humor. [1. Ghosts—Wit and humor. 2. Riddles.] I. Burke, Susan Slattery, ill. II. Title.
PN6371.5.G67   1991   818'.5402—dc20   90-28633
                                                     CIP
Manufactured in the United States of America   AC

1 2 3 4 5 6 7 8 9 10 00 99 98 97 96 95 94 93 92 91

Q: How do you call a skeleton?
A: On the telebone.

Q: What's a favorite ghost dance?
A: Boo-gie woogie.

Q: What goes "crack, crack, whoosh, pop, scared ya"?
A: A ghost chewing booble gum.

Q: How does a skeleton listen to music?
A: He turns on the bone-ograph.

Q: What musical instruments do skeletons play?
A: Trom-bones.

Q: What do witches sing when they mix their brew?

A: "Some Enchanted Evening."

Q: What do ghosts like to eat for dinner?

A: Ham-boo-gers and french fright potatoes.

Q: What do witches like to drink?

A: Apple spider.

Q: What do skeletons like to eat for dinner?

A: Maca-boney and cheese.

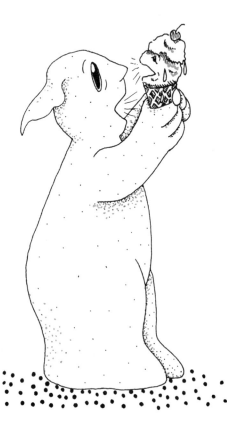

Q: What do ghosts like to drink?
A: Lemoanade.

Q: What do ghosts and goblins
eat for lunch?
A: Peanut boo-ter sand-witches.

Q: What do ghosts like to eat
for dessert?
A: Ice scream.

Q: What did the vampire say when he saw his baby son?

A: "What do we call that new fangled thing?"

Q: How did the mother vampire know her little vampire had a cold?

A: She heard him coffin.

Q: What do baby zombies wear?

A: Die-pers.

Q: Why did the Egyptian ghost cry?

A: She wanted her mummy.

Q: Why wouldn't the little ghost go to sleep?
A: She wanted her night fright turned on.

Q: What do baby ghosts wear on their feet?
A: Booties.

Q: What do little ghosts do before bedtime?
A: They take boo-ble baths.

Q: What does a witch's broom do when it's tired?
A: It goes to sweep.

Q: Why do ghosts hear so well?
A: Because they're eerie.

Q: What did the vampire say
as he slipped into his coffin
at sun up?
A: "I got here in the neck of time."

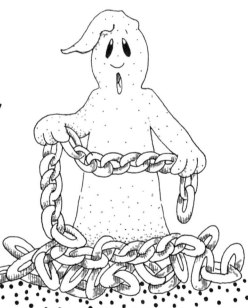

Q: When do ghosts make noise?
A: Every chains they get.

Q: What does a ghost read in bed?

A: A scary boo-k.

Q: Who was the most famous ghost detective?

A: Sherlock Moans.

Q: Who was the most famous witch detective?

A: Warlock Holmes.

Q: Who was the most famous skeleton detective?

A: Sherlock Bones.

Q: What do you call a ghost pirate?
A: A boocaneer.

Q: Who is the most famous French skeleton?
A: Napoleon Bone-aparte .

Q: Which building does Dracula visit in New York?
A: The Vampire State Building.

Q: Where do most goblins live?
A: In North and South Scarolina.

Q: Where do most werewolves live?
A: Howlywood, California.

Q: What do you say to a skeleton leaving on a long cruise?

A: "Bone voyage!"

Q: Where do ghouls stay on vacation?

A: At the gobl-inn.

Q: What do skeletons wear out in the sun?

A: Sun bone-ets.

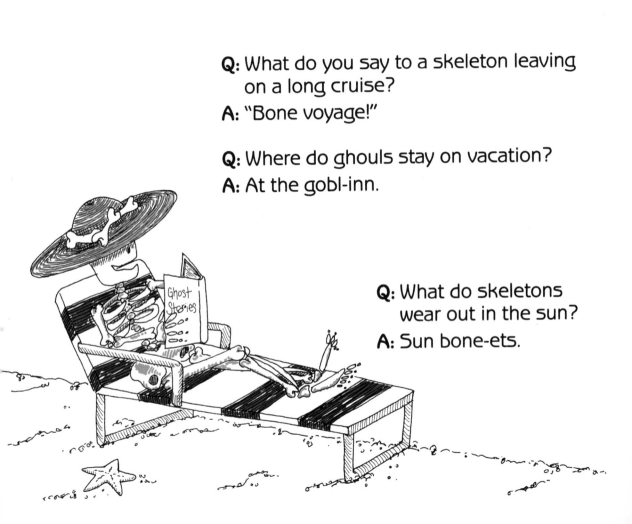

Q: What do you call
a rancher ghost?

A: A boockaroo.

Q: How do ghouls travel?

A: By flying ghost to ghost.

Q: Where do ghosts go
on vacation?

A: Lake Eerie.

Q: Why did the ghost go to the amusement park?

A: To ride the roller ghoster.

Q: What does a ghost do when he gets into a car?

A: He boockles up for safety.

Q: How does an owl stop?

A: It comes to a screeching halt.

Q: How do goblins travel?

A: In troll-ey cars.

Q: What does a ghost use when she runs out of bus tokens?

A: Loose chains.

Q: What do witches do when they are tired?

A: They stop for a spell.

Q: What lawn game do witches play?
A: Crow-quet.

Q: How do witches play baseball?
A: They use their bats.

Q: How do you cheer for an owl?
A: Hip hip hoo hoo hoo ray.

Q: How do witches and ghosts celebrate the Fourth of July?
A: Witches light fire cacklers and ghosts light spooklers.

Q: What subject are witches best at in school?

A: Spelling.

Q: How do ghosts write their names?

A: They en-grave them.

Q: Why did the mad scientist have to learn to be patient?

A: He was too Igor.

Q: What does a nearsighted ghost wear
so he can see?

A: Spooktacles.

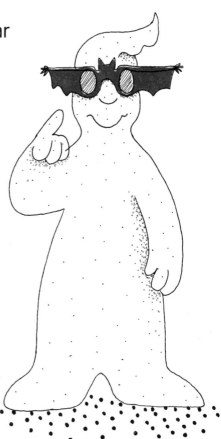

Q: What kind of flowers grow
in ghost gardens?

A: Moaning glories and
morning gories.

Q: What prize did the ghost win at the
fair?

A: A boo ribbon for booberry pie.

Q: What happens when witches look alike?
A: You don't know which witch is which.

Q: What kind of makeup do ghosts wear?
A: Mas-scare-a.

Q: What did the ghost do when he lost his shoe?
A: He haunted for it.

Q: What do you call the furry coats monsters wear?
A: Wolf-were.

Q: What did the witch say about her trip to the beauty shop?

A: It was a hair-raising experience.

Q: When are ghost stores open?

A: Every day Moanday through Frightday.

Q: How do you bargain with a witch?

A: You hag-gle.

Q: Why do witches go to the circus?
A: To see the acro-bats.

Q: Why do skeletons laugh so much?
A: They have funny bones.

Q: How does a ghost open the door of a haunted house?
A: She uses a spookey.

Q: What do you give a skeleton for Valentine's Day?

A: Bone-bones in a heart-shaped box.

Q: What holiday do werewolves like best?

A: Howl-oween.

Q: What is a vampire's favorite holiday?

A: Fangsgiving.

Q: What song do werewolves sing at Christmas?

A: "Deck the Howls with Bow-wows of Howly."

ABOUT THE AUTHORS

What has two heads, four arms, four legs, and laughs a lot? No, not a two-headed, four-armed, four-legged monster with the giggles. It's **Jeffie Ross Gordon**, who is really Judith Ross Enderle and Stephanie Gordon Tessler, southern California authors. They also have two husbands (one each) and six children (three each). They have written many novels and picture books, including *Nora* (Scholastic) and *Six Sleepy Sheep* (Boyds Mills Press). When they're not writing, they teach writing, speak at schools, or hide out in the library where there's no shrieking allowed.

ABOUT THE ARTIST

Susan Slattery Burke loves to illustrate fun-loving characters, especially animals. To her, each of them has a personality all its own. Her satisfaction comes when the characters come to life for the reader as well. Susan lives in Minneapolis, Minnesota, with her husband, their daughter, and their dog and cat. A graduate of the University of Minnesota, Susan enjoys sculpting, travel, illustrating, chasing her daughter, and being outdoors.

If you like **Hide and Shriek**, you'll love these other **You Must Be Joking** riddle books:

Alphabatty: Riddles from A to Z
Help Wanted: Riddles about Jobs
Here's to Ewe: Riddles about Sheep
Ho Ho Ho! Riddles about Santa Claus
I Toad You So: Riddles about Frogs and Toads
On with the Show: Show Me Riddles
Out on a Limb: Riddles about Trees and Plants
That's for Shore: Riddles from the Beach
Weather or Not: Riddles for Rain and Shine
What's Gnu? Riddles from the Zoo
Wing It! Riddles about Birds